SUMO

BIZARRO

Chronicle Books · San Francisco

Elvis in Dallas, 1990

Just as my every breath is dedicated to "Poodlepie", my fabulous wife of more than ten years, so is this book. I owe an immeasurable debt to her for her encouragement and support, and will always remember with great fondness the day she loomed over me and said, "Get a job or I'm leaving you." It was the combination of those words and the blunt object she held above her as she spoke them that gave me the courage and motivation to begin the chain of events that eventually led to my so-called career as a cartoonist.

A debt is also owed to Stan Arnold, a man whose red pen and spelling skills are feared and respected the world over. Thanks to him for his continuing friendship and direction.

Thanks also to Stuart, Jean, Bill, Julie, Mary Ann(e), Killy Willy & Kato Potato and, of course, the Semi-Official Bizarro Canadian Fan Club and Motor Oil Company—Marty, Tony, Mike, John, Ken, Mad Dog Dean & "The King."

3

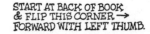

4

7

9

11

13

14

15

19

21

24

THE FASHION CONSENSUS FOR THE NINETIES IS THAT WIDE LAPELS AND TROUSER CUFFS ARE BACK — AND THIS TIME THEY MEAN BUSINESS.

SAY, FELLAS, I JUST RETIRED A COUPLE OF WEEKS AGO. WHERE CAN I GET A GOOD DEAL ON SOME BAGGY SHORTS, A FLOPPY HAT AND A METAL DETECTOR?

32

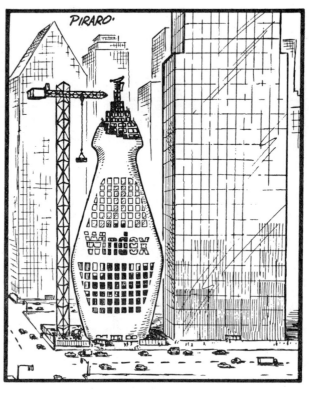

39

42

44

50

55

57

THE DIMINUTIVE, DELICATE GLASS GLOBE PERCHES PRECARIOUSLY HIGH ABOVE THE RIGID CERAMIC FLOOR, HELD IN PLACE BY A SINGLE ROTATION AGAINST THE FORCES OF GRAVITY. A PORTRAIT OF FRAGILITY, IT WAITS PATIENTLY TO UNERRINGLY COMPLETE ITS SINGLE INTENDED PURPOSE — TO SHED A SLIVER OF SHIMMERING LIGHT UPON THE DARK AND DREARY LIVES OF ITS CREATORS...

SHALL I TURN ON THE LAMP, DEAR?

GENTLY.

PIRARO.

I JUST FIGURED IT UP. — IF WE QUIT SMOKING WE WOULD SAVE $12,725⁰⁰ A YEAR.

PIRARO.

59

60

66

78

80

82

84

86

START AT FRONT OF BOOK & FLIP THIS CORNER FORWARD WITH RIGHT THUMB AND LAUGH.

ABOUT THE PERPETRATOR.

DAN PIRARO LIVES THE SORT OF LIFE MOST PEOPLE ONLY DREAM ABOUT. HIS REPUTATION FOR BRAVADO IN THE FACE OF DANGER & INCONVENIENT WEATHER HAS REACHED MYTHICAL PROPORTIONS IN HIS HOME STATE OF TEXAS. LOCAL LEGEND TELLS OF A TIME WHEN HE MARCHED COURAGEOUSLY INTO THE GAPING MOUTH OF A SUPER MARKET WITHOUT ANY INTENTION OF BUYING FOOD. ANOTHER STORY, ROUTINELY TOLD AROUND CAMPSITES ALL OVER NORTH AMERICA, SPEAKS OF PIRARO THE SURVIVOR. WHEN STRANDED BY A BLIZZARD ON THE SIDE OF A STEEP PRECIPICE FOR OVER FORTY MINUTES, HE STAYED ALIVE BY STARTING A FIRE WITH ONLY A GALLON OF GASOLINE, A DISPOSABLE LIGHTER, AND A HUGE PILE OF WOOD.

NOW IN HIS SIXTH YEAR AS THE MOST WIDELY READ CARTOONIST IN THE HISTORY OF HIS HIGHSCHOOL, PIRARO SPENDS HIS DAYS DRAWING, HIS EVENINGS POLISHING SAUSAGES, AND CAN OFTEN BE HEARD LAUGHING MANIACALLY FROM THE BASEMENT OF HIS DARKENED HOME WELL INTO THE NIGHT.

ABOUT HIS WIFE.

I WOULD LIKE TO MAKE A SPECIAL ACKNOWLEDGEMENT TO KALIN BURKE PIRARO, WHO IS ALL TOO OFTEN REFERRED TO IN THE ABOVE MANNER. SHE IS ESPECIALLY CLEVER, KNOWLEDGEABLE & INTUITIVE IN MANY AREAS AND CASTS THE DECIDING VOTE WHENEVER I REACH AN IMPASSE. TWO IMPORTANT EXAMPLES WOULD BE THE LAST TWO BOOK COVERS. WHEN STUCK FOR A VISUAL FOR THE TITLE GLASNOST BIZARRO (A TITLE DREAMED UP BY DREW MONTGOMERY AT CHRONICLE BOOKS) SHE SUGGESTED THE CONCEPT OF FOREIGN LANGUAGE CAPTIONS & THE COSSACK AND TOURISTS IN RED SQUARE. ON THIS BOOK, THE TITLE SUMO BIZARRO & THE CHOICE OF WHICH EXSISTING CARTOON TO USE WERE ENTIRELY HER IDEA. I, ON THE OTHER HAND, HAVE NEVER TITLED ONE OF MY OWN BOOKS, BEING PERFECTLY CONTENT TO LET KALIN DO ALL THE WORK WHILE I BASK IN HER RADIANCE.